TUDOR
1485–1603

STUART
1603–1714

VICTORIAN
1837–1901

MODERN TIMES
1901–NOW

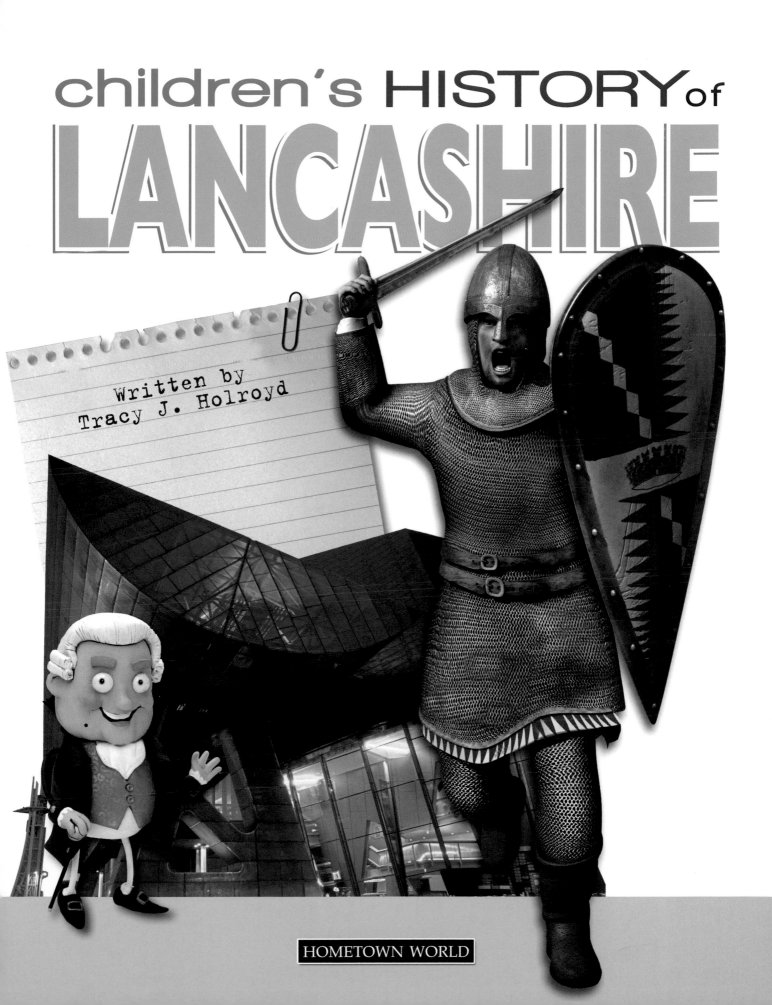

children's HISTORY of
LANCASHIRE

Written by
Tracy J. Holroyd

HOMETOWN WORLD

How well do you know Lancashire?

Have you ever wondered what it would have been like living in Lancashire when the Romans arrived? What about going to see Blackpool Tower when it was new? This book will uncover the important and exciting things that happened in this wonderful county.

Some rather brainy folk have worked on this book to make sure it's fun and informative. So what are you waiting for? Peel back the pages and be amazed at Lancashire's very own story.

'Spot this!' game with hints on something to find in the county

THE FACTS

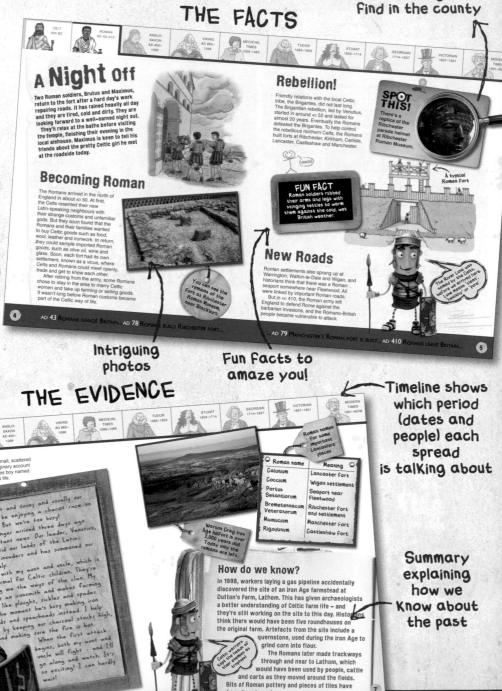

Intriguing photos

Fun facts to amaze you!

THE EVIDENCE

Imaginary account of what it was like for children growing up in Lancashire

Timeline shows which period (dates and people) each spread is talking about

Summary explaining how we know about the past

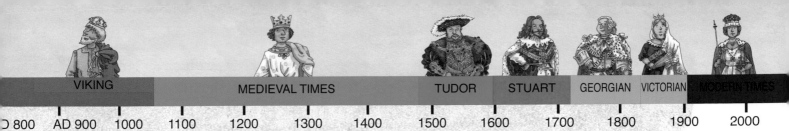

Contents

A Night off

Two Roman soldiers, Brutus and Maximus, return to the fort after a hard day's work repairing roads. It has rained heavily all day and they are tired, cold and dirty. They are looking forward to a well-earned night out. They'll relax at the baths before visiting the temple, finishing their evening in the local alehouse. Maximus is keen to tell his friends about the pretty Celtic girl he met at the roadside today.

Becoming Roman

The Romans arrived in the north of England in about AD 50. At first, the Celts resented their new Latin-speaking neighbours with their strange customs and unfamiliar gods. But they soon found that the Romans and their families wanted to buy Celtic goods such as food, wool, leather and ironwork. In return, they could sample imported Roman goods, such as olive oil, wine and glass. Soon, each fort had its own settlement, known as a vicus, where Celts and Romans could meet openly, trade and get to know each other.

After retiring from the army, some Romans chose to stay in the area to marry Celtic women and take up farming or selling goods. It wasn't long before Roman customs became part of the Celtic way of life.

You can see the remains of the fort at Ribchester Roman Museum, near Blackburn.

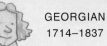
Rebellion!

Friendly relations with the local Celtic tribe, the Brigantes, did not last long. The Brigantian rebellion, led by Venutius, started in around AD 52 and lasted for almost 20 years. Eventually the Romans defeated the Brigantes. To help control the rebellious northern Celts, the Romans built forts at Ribchester, Kirkham, Carlisle, Lancaster, Castleshaw and Manchester.

SPOT THIS! There's a replica of the Ribchester parade helmet at Ribchester Roman Museum.

ouch!

FUN FACT
Roman soldiers rubbed their arms and legs with stinging nettles to warm them against the cold, wet British weather.

A typical Roman fort

New Roads

Roman settlements also sprang up at Warrington, Walton-le-Dale and Wigan, and historians think that there was a Roman seaport somewhere near Fleetwood. All were linked by important Roman roads.

But in AD 410, the Roman army left England to defend Rome against the barbarian invasions, and the Romano-British people became vulnerable to attack.

The River Lune was named by the Celts before we arrived here. Lune means clean, healthy or pure.

...AD 79 MANCHESTER'S ROMAN FORT IS BUILT... AD 410 ROMANS LEAVE BRITAIN...

5

CELT
500 BC

ROMAN
AD 43–410

ANGLO-
SAXON
AD 450–
1066

VIKING
AD 865–
1066

MEDIEVA
TIMES
1066–148

The Brigantes lived in small, scattered settlements. In the imaginary account below, a young Brigantes boy named Judoc tells us about his life.

You're not putting my head on a gatepost, you Celtic clown!

Today is hot and sunny and usually our tribe would be enjoying a chariot race on the beach. But we're too busy!

A messenger arrived three days ago with important news. Our leader, Venutius, plans to rid our lands of the Latin-speaking invaders and has summoned our tribe's help.

I live with my aunt and uncle, which is quite normal for Celtic children. They're teaching me the ways of the clan. My uncle is an ironsmith and makes farming tools like ploughs, sickles and spades. At the moment he's busy making iron swords and spearheads instead. I help him by keeping our charcoal stocks high, and making sure the fire is hot.

When the first attack begins, both my aunt and uncle will fight – and I'll go along and watch. It's so exciting! I can hardly wait!

Roman names for some important Lancashire places

Roman name	Meaning
Calunium	Lancaster fort
Coccium	Wigan settlement
Portus Setantiorum	Seaport near Fleetwood
Bremetennacum Veteranorum	Ribchester fort and settlement
Mamucium	Manchester fort
Rigodunum	Castleshaw fort

Warton Crag Iron Age hillfort is over 2,000 years old! Today only the remains are left.

Celtic warriors kept the heads of their enemies as trophies!

How do we know?

In 1998, workers laying a gas pipeline accidentally discovered the site of an Iron Age farmstead at Dutton's Farm, Lathom. This has given archaeologists a better understanding of Celtic farm life – and they're still working on the site to this day. Historians think there would have been five roundhouses on the original farm. Artefacts from the site include a quernstone, used during the Iron Age to grind corn into flour.

The Romans later made trackways through and near to Lathom, which would have been used by people, cattle and carts as they moved around the fields. Bits of Roman pottery and pieces of tiles have been found nearby.

CELT 500 BC	ROMAN AD 43–410	ANGLO-SAXON AD 450–1066	VIKING AD 865–1066	MEDIEVAL TIMES 1066–148

The Defenders

A small Northumbrian force has crossed the Mercian border to steal land. A Saxon boy watches from the trees as his people battle to defend their territory. War cries and the sound of clashing swords fill the air. The battle is fierce and the ground is red with blood. The boy's father is somewhere in the chaos, but he can't see him. He is desperately afraid.

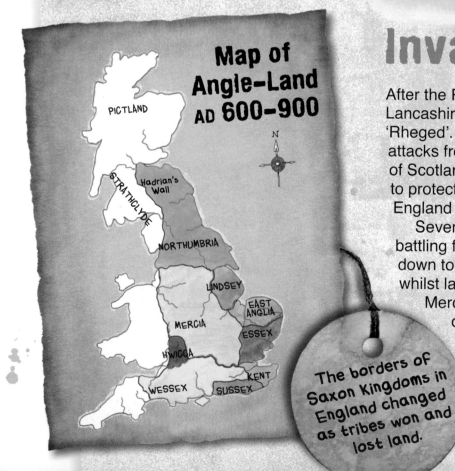

Map of Angle-Land AD 600–900

PICTLAND

STRATHCLYDE

Hadrian's Wall

NORTHUMBRIA

LINDSEY

MERCIA

EAST ANGLIA

ESSEX

HWICCA

KENT

WESSEX

SUSSEX

The borders of Saxon Kingdoms in England changed as tribes won and lost land.

Invaders!

After the Romans left, many forts fell into disrepair. Lancashire became part of a huge kingdom called 'Rheged'. Mostly farmers, the locals struggled against attacks from sea-raiders – mainly the fierce Picts of Scotland. Some probably hired Saxon soldiers to protect them. But eventually, the Saxons took England for themselves.

Several kingdoms made up Saxon England, all battling for control. Land from the Scottish border down to the River Ribble became Northumbria, whilst land to the south of Northumbria became Mercia. Ordinary people built high walls and deep ditches to protect their lands from other Saxon kingdoms. They kept their weapons close by, ready to do battle for their own king at any moment.

By the 7th century, a new people had settled in Lancashire – Norsemen thrown out of Ireland. Anglo-Saxon life was changing.

...AD **429** SAXONS SETTLE...AD **630** CHURCH BUILT ON SITE OF LANCASTER PRIORY...

Religion

Christianity arrived in England during the 7th century. In AD 630, an early church was built where the Lancaster Priory now stands. By AD 850, the Parish of Whalley was the second biggest in England. Churches were built in many other towns around the same time, including Burnley, Bolton and Hornby. Anglo-Saxon Lancashire was growing!

...and deliver us from the Norsemen.

FUN FACT
Saxon buildings were made from wattle and daub – wood and clay mixed with animal poo!

The 'Angel Stone' is a Saxon carving inside Manchester Cathedral. It's over 1,400 years old!

SPOT THIS!
Try to find this Anglo-Saxon cross shaft in the grounds of St Peter's Church, Heysham.

A New Threat

Lancashire suffered badly from Viking raids. In AD 870, Vikings sailed up the Mersey and destroyed Manchester and, by AD 874, Mercia was Danish. Saxon King Alfred the Great waged a campaign against the Danes, and began to win back land.

By the end of the 9th century, the Saxons had regained both Mercia and Viking Northumbria, building fortified settlements to defend themselves against Jorvik – Viking York. As a gesture of peace, King Ethelred gave Irish Norsemen land on the Fylde coast, but the bloodshed continued.

These dangerous times didn't last forever. Eventually, the Saxons and Vikings learned to live together.

...AD 800 VIKINGS INVADE HEYSHAM...AD 870 THE GREAT VIKING INVASION...

9

When the Vikings invaded, the Anglo-Saxons had become Christian. But the Vikings worshipped many gods. Let Sveinn, a young Viking boy, tell you about them in this imaginary account.

I'd like to be strong and brave, like Thor.

The Anglo-Saxons are a strange people. They worship only one God who preaches forgiveness and peace. We Vikings have many gods and they are all mighty warriors. They live in Asgard, where they are ruled by Odin, the All-Father.

Odin has many sons, but my favourite is the Thunder God, Thor, whose mighty hammer, Mjolnir, can summon the storm. Thor has no equal in battle. When I grow up, I want to be just like him!

Even though the Anglo-Saxon God preaches peace, that doesn't stop his people fighting. My Father says that the battle for our land was bloody and hard-fought. But now the Saxon king says we can keep these lands if we promise to stop our attacks.

My Father is glad as he is weary of battle and wants only to farm his land in peace. But my uncle says that the Saxon king's offer proves that he is weak – and we should take what we can!

The Norse hogback stone dates from the year 1000. You can find it inside St Peter's Church, Heysham.

Mighty Odin, grant me the honour of a warrior's death!

The Rock Hewn Graves of St Patrick's Chapel are examples of early Christian burials.

The Vikings were great sailors and brought wealth to Lancashire by trading with Ireland and Europe.

How do we know?

Workmen digging in Lancashire in 1840 discovered a lead-lined chest. When it was prised open, the chest revealed over 8,500 silver coins, ingots and pieces of jewellery. Known today as the Cuerdale Hoard, historians think this treasure belonged to Vikings who were forced out of Ireland in AD 902. Why didn't they ever return to claim their treasure? The few written records that survive from this time are almost all created by early Christian monks. Scribes and monks kept a written record of England, year by year, called the 'Anglo-Saxon Chronicle'.

Building a Castle

The Norman baron oversees the building of his motte and bailey castle. His men have built a mound of earth – the motte – and are now constructing a wooden tower on top. This will become the bailey, which will be the baron's home. Everyone else will live inside the fenced area at the base of the motte, guarding animals, food and equipment. The castle will have two ditches for protection and the baron's men will patrol his lands to make sure the rebellious locals obey him. Those Saxons and Vikings must know their place!

Wait for me, King William! I'll help you control those northern rebels!

FUN FACT
A Saxon 'hundred' was large enough to provide land for 100 families.

Northern Rebels

The Normans invaded England in 1066 but struggled to control the northern rebels. To combat this, William the Conqueror himself led the northern campaign, known as the 'Harrying of the North', eventually destroying most of Saxon Northumbria.

In 1072, William granted land between the Ribble and the Mersey to one of his noblemen, Roger de Poitou. At a later date, William II added Lonsdale, Cartmel and Furness. The county was split into six areas, called 'hundreds'. De Poitou based himself in Lancaster, building a castle on the site of the old Roman fort. But in 1102, he rebelled against King Henry I, and was stripped of his lands.

TUDOR
1485–1603

STUART
1603–1714

GEORGIAN
1714–1837

VICTORIAN
1837–1901

MODERN
TIMES
1901–NOW

A New County

Lancashire became a county around 1168, with Lancaster as its ruling town. In 1267, Edmund Crouchback became the first Earl of Lancaster. But in 1351, Edward III promoted the Earldom to a Dukedom, ensuring that the Duke could now run Lancaster without interference from the king. In 1362, Edward's own son, John of Gaunt, became Duke of Lancaster.

The Tudor Rose is a mixture of the Red Rose of Lancaster and the White Rose of York.

Wars of the Roses

Descendants of the Duke of Lancaster went on to become kings of England: Henry IV, Henry V and Henry VI. Henry IV declared that the title 'Duke of Lancaster' would pass forever to the reigning monarch of England. Unfortunately the neighbouring House of York also believed it had a claim to the throne and civil war broke out between the Houses of Lancaster and York. These 'Wars of the Roses' lasted about 30 years.

Eventually Henry Tudor – another of Lancaster's descendants – won and became King Henry VII in 1485. Henry married Elizabeth of York, uniting the two northern Roses to form the mighty House of Tudor.

Market Time

During the 12th and 13th centuries, towns needed Royal permission to hold a market. Some towns such as Bolton, Wigan, Manchester, Burnley, Preston, Kirkham and Lancaster, grew important enough to hold official markets. But many other towns held them unofficially.

Before 1550, records show at least 40 markets throughout Lancashire. Manchester, Preston and Lancaster also held annual fairs. Despite all of this trade, Lancashire was one of England's poorest counties. It had a small population so didn't generate a lot of tax compared with other counties.

Flemish weavers settled in Manchester in 1363 and the textile trade began to flourish!

How do we know?

In 1086, William the Conqueror sent his men throughout England to make a record of buildings, fields, forests, animals and farmlands. This was called the Domesday Book and still survives today.

Closing the Monasteries

The monks at Furness are praying that their beautiful abbey will be saved but it is too late. Henry VIII has ordered his men to destroy it, along with all of the monasteries and abbeys in the land. The king's soldiers smash the windows to take the coloured glass, and steal all the riches they can lay their hands on. Soon there will be nothing left.

Dissolution

Following his creation of the Church of England in 1534, King Henry VIII began closing down, or 'dissolving', the monasteries. Between 1536 and 1539, Lancashire lost Cartmel Priory, Furness Abbey, Preston Friary, Cockersand Abbey, and many others.

Boys from rich families who had been educated at the monasteries now had nowhere to go. So, during the 16th century, several grammar schools were established throughout Lancashire. These were often paid for by wealthy local gentlemen. Hugh Oldham built Manchester Grammar in 1515 and, in 1653, money from the will of Humphrey Chetham built Chetham's Hospital School for poor boys.

FUN FACT
Girls didn't go to school at this time because they were expected to get married, do housework and have children.

Witches on Trial

In Tudor and Stuart times, some people made money from claiming they had powers in witchcraft. This was illegal and, in 1612, the Lancashire Witch Trials took place at Lancaster Castle. Nineteen local people were charged with witchcraft, including the ill-fated Alice Nutter and the Pendle Witches from Pendle Forest. Most of them were hanged for their crime. One of the so-called witches, Old Mother Chattox, was accused of robbing graveyards, where she stole teeth from skeletons to help with her spells!

Civil War

In 1642, the English Civil War began, and supporters of the king fought supporters of Parliament. Lancashire was mostly Royalist, supporting King Charles I. But some towns, such as Manchester and Bolton, were strongly Parliamentarian, supporting Cromwell and his 'Roundheads'. During the siege of Manchester in 1642, the Royalists demanded weapons and men for the king. They were met with the shout "No men, no arms, not even a rusty dagger!"

The 1648 Battle of Preston, fought on Ribbleton Moor and led by Cromwell himself, was a landmark victory for the Roundheads, destroying King Charles I's grip on the north. Royalist volunteers who survived the battle were sent to plantations in Barbados and Virginia as slaves! The Civil War ended with Parliament's victory in 1648 and, in 1649, King Charles was executed.

Some people say this is Alice Nutter's grave but the dates are wrong. Also, witches weren't allowed to be buried in churchyards.

SPOT THIS!

Can you find the Nutter family grave at St Mary's Church in Newchurch-in-Pendle?

With religious disputes and civil war, Lancashire was an unsettled place to live in Tudor and Stuart times.

How do we know?

John Leland travelled around the country in Tudor times and wrote an account of what he saw. A pioneering female traveller called Celia Fiennes kept a diary as she rode around England in the late 17th century. Other important documents, such as Humphrey Chetham's will, also still exist today. The true story of the trial of the Lancashire Witches was documented by a clerk called Thomas Potts. In 1613, this was published as a book, entitled 'The Wonderfull Discoverie of Witches in the Countie of Lancaster'.

New Canals

It is a hot summer's day. An old barge horse plods steadily along the towpath, pulling a heavy barge on the new canal. The barge is loaded up with coal from the mines in Worsley. The canal boy, Thomas, tugs gently on the horse's reins, reassuring him that it's not far to go now. The horse grunts and slowly walks on.

Revolution!

Much of Lancashire's trade had once relied on the woollen and linen industry. But, by 1750, cotton was more popular than wool. Lancashire was perfect for processing cotton due to its damp climate, and had no shortage of skilled spinners and weavers.

The machinery of the industrial revolution produced textiles quickly. Mills and warehouses shot up, turning hundreds of small villages – especially in east Lancashire – into industrialised towns. Lancashire's powerful streams turned mill waterwheels, and later, its coal provided fuel for mill steam engines. Manchester acted as the main trading centre, opening a cotton exchange in 1729.

Thousands of people migrated into places like Manchester and Bolton in search of a better life. Sadly, many people found themselves in even worse conditions.

You can see an original mill engine in motion inside the Engine House at Oak Mount Mill in Burnley.

...1714 GEORGE I BECOMES KING...1729 MANCHESTER COTTON EXCHANGE OPENS...

TUDOR 1485–1603	STUART 1603–1714	GEORGIAN 1714–1837	VICTORIAN 1837–1901	MODERN TIMES 1901–NOW

Better Transport

The new industrial towns needed a more efficient transport system. By 1736, the Irwell and Mersey were navigable, so barges from Manchester could reach the Liverpool docks. Cheap coal was needed to power the mills, so the Duke of Bridgewater instructed an engineer called James Brindley to build a canal to import coal from the Worsley mines. This took the form of the Bridgewater Canal, which opened in 1761.

A network of canals quickly followed – the Leeds and Liverpool Canal, the Manchester, Bolton and Bury Canal, and the Ashton, Rochdale and Lancaster canals. But canal barges were slow, and something faster was needed. In 1830, the country's first intercity railway opened from Manchester to Liverpool. The age of the locomotive had begun! People could travel further and faster than ever before. This was an exciting time in Lancashire.

Coal was loaded onto barges at Worsley and shipped out on the Bridgewater Canal.

Georgian times were named after four kings called George. This is George III.

Towns such as Wigan, Bolton and Salford became known as 'Little Manchesters'. How wonderful!

Crucial Coal

Lancashire also enjoyed a booming coal industry, thanks to its rich coal deposits. Many coal dynasties were born, including the Hultons of Hulton Park and the Bradshaighs of Haigh Hall in Wigan. The pit owners grew rich, whilst workers – including women and children – worked in dire conditions, picking coal by hand.

Children as young as five were forced to sit in the dark, waiting to open ventilation doors for miners. Thankfully, the 1842 Mines Act banned boys under the age of 10, and women and girls, from working underground.

Trading Places

Port towns such as Lancaster, Preston and Liverpool had trade links with Europe, North America and the West Indies. They exported woollen goods, coal, tools and machinery, and imported hemp, iron, timber, sugar, tobacco, rum and raw cotton. Lancaster had sugar processing and shipbuilding industries, and manufactured candles, ropes and sailcloth.

Improvements

Lancashire had its first newspapers, hospitals and theatres in Georgian times. Many towns opened dispensaries where poor people could get free medicine. Special committees were set up to make improvements, such as building roads and cleaning streets. They also replaced the oil-fuelled street lighting with gas. In 1792, nightwatchmen began patrolling the streets of Manchester and Salford in an effort to tackle crime. This proved so popular that many other towns followed.

Robert Gillow became famous for producing furniture in Lancaster.

Raging Riots

One of the 'men' hanged for attacking the Westhoughton mill was only 12 years old.

Before the Industrial Revolution, handloom weavers worked in their own homes to produce cloth. The development of new textile machinery at first helped them to work faster. But as technology quickly advanced, the machines began to take over, putting people out of work. Desperate to stop the advance of the machines, the weavers took drastic action.

In 1812, a mob trashed and burned a Westhoughton mill. Four men were later convicted and hanged for taking part. Trouble continued and, in April 1826, a huge mob set out from Whinney Hill, near Accrington, to destroy mills at Over Darwen, Helmshore and Blackburn. Eventually, to end the unrest, the army opened fire, killing four people.

Massacre!

Although Lancashire had grown very quickly, very few people were allowed to vote and Manchester had no Members of Parliament. On 16th August 1819, Henry Hunt held a meeting in St Peter's Fields to do something about this. Around 80,000 people joined him, but the local government sent armed cavalry to move them on. The cavalry charged into the crowd, slashing with sabres. Fifteen people died and 600 lay injured. This was called the 'Peterloo Massacre'.

Painting of the Peterloo Massacre

FUN FACT
Prince Louis Napoleon lived on Lord Street in Southport during his exile. He returned to France in 1851 to become Emperor Louis Napoleon III.

Sir Robert Peel was born in Bury and created the first modern police force.

Poverty

Living conditions in larger towns such as Manchester and Preston were horrendous. Families lived in damp, overcrowded houses. Up to 12 people shared a room, taking turns to use the beds. Many slept on filthy straw in slime-coated cellars. The toilet was often just a hole in the ground.

Human and household waste was dumped in rivers and open sewers, or on the streets. Diseases such as typhoid and cholera were rife, and thousands of people died. To make matters worse, food became so expensive that many of the poor starved.

SPOT THIS!

Can you find this statue of Sir Robert Peel in Manchester's Piccadilly Gardens? There's a statue of him in Bury, too.

Not everyone in Georgian Lancashire lived a life of misery and hardship. Let William explain.

This Georgian street in Liverpool shows the kind of house William might have lived in.

I'm William, and I live in a rich part of Preston with my mother, father and sister. Our street is full of elegant, terraced homes, each with three floors, a basement and an attic.

My father is a banker, so we have lots of visitors and need many servants. We have a butler, a cook, a lady's maid, an upstairs maid, two footmen and a scullery maid.

Our town is known as 'Proud Preston' because of all the wealthy people who live here. But some parts of Preston are dirty and horrid. Those places are where the mill workers live.

In hot weather, we can actually smell the slums from our street. My father forbids us to go anywhere near them, because they are full of disease. He also says there are rats as big as cats!

The elegant Rodney Street in Liverpool is nicknamed the 'Harley Street of the North'.

A statue of the inventor Samuel Crompton sits in his hometown, Bolton.

Evidence of Georgian Lancashire is everywhere!

How do we know?

In the Castlefield area of Manchester you can walk among Georgian mills and warehouses. Meanwhile, textile machinery is displayed at Manchester's Museum of Science and Industry, including Kay's Flying Shuttle, Hargreaves' Spinning Jenny and Cartwright's Power Loom. The only surviving Spinning Mule built by Crompton is on display at Bolton Museum.

Oak Mount Mill produced cotton until 1979 and was one of the last steam-powered mills in Burnley to close. Today the engine is operated by an electric motor.

By the mid 19th century, Lancashire's cotton industry was the biggest in the world!

Samuel Crompton invented the Spinning Mule in 1779 but was never paid for it. He died in poverty in 1827.

21

A Day Out

It is August 1871 and everyone at the station is waiting for the arrival of the steam train to Southport. They are excited about riding on a train and having the bank holiday off from work, far from the dark smog of the factory town. At Southport, they will walk along the promenade and pier, and picnic on the sands. They will enjoy clear views of the sea and breathe in fresh, salty air. If it gets really hot, some of them may even take a swim!

Poo!

Our ash-pit privy is a metal pail in a box with a wooden seat on top. We use ash from the fire to cover any mess but it still stinks!

FUN FACT
In his book, 'Hard Times', Charles Dickens based the fictional city of Coketown on Preston.

Poor Lancashire

Most people in Victorian Lancashire still lived in horrific poverty – especially those in the larger, more crowded towns. Poor people still died young and few babies survived. However, the Victorians tried to improve living conditions, with towns like Manchester and Preston leading the way.

From the 1850s, towns acquired sewers, piped water supplies and cemeteries in which to bury their dead. Even so, there were few flush toilets and, by the early 19th century, many people still used ash-pit privies as loos, with the nightsoil cart taking away the waste.

Trade is Good

The iron, coal, slate and salt industries flourished, as did the textile industry. Lancaster began to produce linoleum and oilcloth, and Liverpool grew to be the second most important port in the country.

Trade was helped by improved transport. A network of railways spread throughout Lancashire, arriving at Preston in 1838 and Blackburn in 1846. The railways also allowed Victorians to travel quickly to seaside resorts, such as Southport, Blackpool and Morecambe, where it became fashionable to holiday by the sea. In 1894, Daniel Adamson constructed the Manchester Ship Canal, linking its docks in Salford to the sea.

Southport Pier is the second longest pier in Britain. This photo shows the Pier in 1902.

Lord Ashton built this in memory of his wife. Sob!

Leisure Time

From the 1840s, towns created parks so that people could enjoy fresh air and exercise. James Williamson paid for Williamson Park to be created on the site of Lancaster Moor's old stone quarries. His son, also called James Williamson, ensured the park was completed. The younger James Williamson became a millionaire from producing oilcloth and linoleum, and was later named Lord Ashton.

In 1824, John Dalton helped found a Mechanics' Institute in Manchester, where working-class men could take evening classes. In 1891, Sir Thomas Storey gave the Lancaster people art and technical schools and a library called The Storey Institute. Museums and art galleries also shot up, including Preston's Harris Museum and Art Gallery.

SPOT THIS!

Have you ever been to Williamson Park? Look out for the Ashton Memorial, built by Lord Ashton.

For many of the Lancashire Victorians, holiday time meant a trip to one of the local seaside towns. Ten-year-old Ria wants to tell you about her trip to Blackpool.

People say that the tower in Paris is even bigger than the one in Blackpool!

My Ma, Pa, brother and I are going to Blackpool for a week's holiday. We've been there before but this time we're really excited because we're going to see the new Blackpool Tower! Pa says the first one to spot it from the train window wins a penny!

When we finally arrive, we'll go straight to the beach, where we'll search for crabs and shells and build sandcastles. We'll ride on donkeys and watch a Punch and Judy show. For lunch, we'll buy tubs of cockles and mussels or periwinkles. Delicious!

Tomorrow, Pa will take us to the Pleasure Beach, where we'll get to ride on the merry-go-rounds. If it rains we'll probably go to the Winter Gardens instead. Best of all will be our visit to the Tower Circus. People say it has the greatest acrobats, jugglers and clowns in the world, and even performing animals like dogs, horses and elephants! Gosh, I've never seen an elephant before!

Blackpool Tower opened in 1894. It was designed by James Maxwell and Charles Tuke from Manchester.

FUN FACT

The Mayor of Blackpool loved the Eiffel Tower in Paris so much that he decided Blackpool should have a tower of its own!

At Crich Tramway Village in Derbyshire you can see one of Blackpool's original electric trams from 1885.

6ᴰ **WINTER GARDENS** 6ᴰ
ONE CONTINUOUS ROUND OF ENTERTAINMENT ALL DAY

How do we know?

The writings of Friedrich Engels, Elizabeth Gaskell and Charles Dickens describe the horrific conditions in which the people of the large cotton towns lived. You can find original Victorian mill buildings and warehouses in the Weavers' Triangle at Burnley, and its Visitor Centre contains original documents, photographs and objects from the mills.

At seaside resorts such as Blackpool, Morecambe and Southport, you can find Victorian buildings everywhere – piers, hotels and dance halls. Blackpool's North Pier opened in 1863 and is a great example of Victorian architecture.

Lancashire grew quickly in Victorian times because of its mills and other industries.

25

Evacuate!

Alfie and Jane have been evacuated from Salford to Haslingden, carrying only their gas masks and a few belongings. The cardboard labels tied to their coat buttons reveal their names, addresses and ages. They are confused and unhappy because they did not want to leave their families and friends, but the grown-ups believe that it's too dangerous for them to stay. But they would rather have stayed at home than come to this strange place.

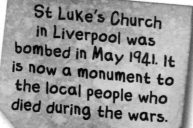

St Luke's Church in Liverpool was bombed in May 1941. It is now a monument to the local people who died during the wars.

Big Changes

After World War One, Lancashire saw huge changes as the cotton industry began to collapse. Some places, like Preston, suffered mass unemployment, but gradually new industries in engineering and manufacturing sprang up. The Great Depression of the 1930s brought further hardship, with a severe shortage of jobs and money throughout all Lancashire.

World War Two

During World War Two, the German air force bombed Liverpool, Manchester and Barrow-in-Furness heavily, as they were all key players in the war effort. Manchester was a big manufacturing city, and especially important was its production of war planes at the Avro aircraft factory. The ports of Liverpool, Wallasey Pool and Bootle imported vital goods and welcomed allied ships, whereas Barrow was an important builder of warships.

The Blitz

'The Blitz' was the name given to the bombing raids of 1940 and 1941. Liverpool, Bootle and Wirral took the brunt of the bombings, with over 4,000 people killed. Sometimes the German bombers would miss their targets, or unload unused bombs as they flew across Lancashire on their way home, so many places suffered bomb damage.

SPOT THIS!

Where can you find the 'Messenger of Peace'? Try looking in Manchester's Peace Garden.

New Industries

It's been a hard day's night and I've been working like a... cat?

After World War Two, Barrow's mining and steel-making industry declined, leaving it reliant on its shipyards. In the 1950s, Liverpool's industries and docks also went into decline but the city rallied again during the 1960s as it became home to the 'Mersey beat' – the sound of pop music by The Beatles, Cilla Black and a host of others. In Lancaster, furniture production ceased, and the river silted up, causing major problems for its port industry. For some time, things looked bad for Lancashire as the old industries faded. But successful industries, such as linoleum production and engineering, ensured that the county was reborn. Meanwhile the music scene in Manchester grew, producing bands such as Oasis and pop groups such as Take That.

Moving Borders

By 1974, Lancashire had become a huge county. The government decided to change the boundaries for setting council tax and other services. Although traditional boundaries stayed the same, many Lancashire towns became part of new counties such as Merseyside, Cumbria and Greater Manchester. Lancashire also gained districts from West Yorkshire. Since then the counties have altered again, causing great confusion. However, the traditional county of Lancashire still stretches from the River Mersey in the south to the River Duddon in the north.

After the war, the mines closed down. Today, we have oil rigs and wind farms instead.

Today and Tomorrow

Lancashire's future is bright – mostly thanks to its often murky past! It is literally one huge museum and leisure centre, packed with gripping stories, rich heritage and exciting places to visit.

⬆ First opened in 1896, Blackpool Pleasure Beach is now Britain's number one tourist attraction! Will it still be as popular for tourists in 2096?

The Lowry Arts Centre on Salford Quays celebrates the artist L. S. Lowry, who was born in Stretford in Lancashire in 1887. He made Salford famous with his paintings. ➡

⬆ Lancaster Castle stands on a hilltop dominating Lancaster city's skyline. Its history can be traced back almost 1,000 years.

SPOT THIS!

Can you spot this statue of Morecambe's famous comedian on Morecambe Promenade?

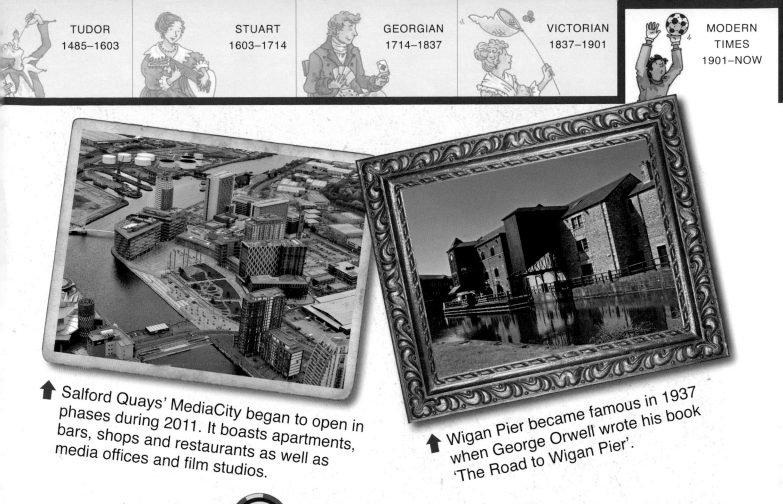

↑ Salford Quays' MediaCity began to open in phases during 2011. It boasts apartments, bars, shops and restaurants as well as media offices and film studios.

↑ Wigan Pier became famous in 1937 when George Orwell wrote his book 'The Road to Wigan Pier'.

People from Lancashire are known as Lancastrians. You should feel proud to be a Lancastrian!

How will they know?

How will future generations know about our Lancashire? Historically and geographically, Lancashire is linked to two very important cities: Manchester and Salford. Manchester is famous around the world for its football, music, architecture and science while Salford, with its own rich Lancashire heritage, will become world-famous as home to MediaCity.

By 2016, Lancashire aims to be attracting 85 million visitors every year. Tourists armed with digital cameras and access to the Internet will ensure that the evidence will survive for all to see.

Glossary

Abbey – a building where monks or nuns live and work.

AD – a short way to write anno Domini, which is Latin and means 'in the year of Our Lord', i.e. after the birth of Christ.

Allied – a word often used in times of war, meaning friendly (on the same side as us).

Archaeologist – a person who studies the past by examining buildings and objects left behind by previous people and cultures.

Artefact – a word often used for an archaeological object.

Asgard – said to be the name of the place where the Norse Gods, such as Thor and Odin, lived.

Cholera – a deadly disease caused by filthy water.

Christianity – the name of the religion whose followers believe Jesus Christ is the son of God.

Church of England – a Christian religion headed by the king or queen. King Henry VIII started this religion, with himself as the head of it.

Civil war – this is a war where people in the same country fight each other.

Committee – a group of people who get together, make official decisions and get things done.

Customs – traditions and ways of life used by different societies.

Dispensary – a place where medicine is handed out.

Evacuate – having to leave your home and live somewhere else for safety.

Export – take goods made in this country and sell them in another country.

Fort or **fortress** – a large, strong building offering military support and protection.

Import – buy goods from another country and sell them in this country.

Latin – the language used in ancient Rome and the foundation of many other languages.

Monastery – a place where monks live and worship.

Monk – a male member of a religious community that has to live by rules such as poverty and obedience.

Parliamentarian – anyone who fought on the side of Oliver Cromwell and Parliament in the English Civil War. Also known as a Roundhead.

Port – a place at the edge of land where the water is deep enough for ships to stay.

Priory – a religious house that is similar to an Abbey but may be smaller.

Promenade – a paved road, often at the seaside, where people can go for a walk.

Quarry – a large area of land where stone is dug or blasted out of the ground.

Quernstone – another name for a mill stone, a small circular stone used for grinding corn.

Royalist – anyone who fought on the side of King Charles I in the English Civil War. Also known as a Cavalier.

Scribe – a person who made handwritten copies of books, before printing was invented.

Tram – a form of transport that was attached to overhead electric cables and ran on rails dug into in the streets.

Weaver – a person who makes cloth from wool.

Index

Acknowledgements

The author would like to thank the following people for their generous help:
My brother, David, whose name should be on the cover of this book alongside my own. Thank you for your fantastic story ideas, and for all the hours you spent helping me to write and revise the manuscript. Also, thanks to Mum and Dad, Barbara and Ronnie, for cheerfully bearing with their obsessive offspring. Thanks to June Jones for the loan of her local history books, and to Salix Homes Limited for kindly offering access to its extensive archives.

The publishers would like to thank the following people and organizations
for their permission to reproduce material on the following pages:
p1: Paul Reid/Shutterstock; p4: Immanuel Giel/Wikipedia; p5: Rex Harris/Wikipedia; p7: Steven Glover/Flickr; p9: Manchester Cathedral, John Burke; p10: John Burke; p11: John Burke; p13: Ale flashero/Wikipedia; p15: Hayley Hardman/Flickr; p16: www.iknow-northwest.co.uk; p18: ©Tatton Park/Cheshire East Council/National Trust, photographed by George Littler and Peter Spooner; p19: Manchester Archives and Local Studies; p20: Paul Holloway/Flickr; p21: Terry Whalebone/Flickr, Bolton Museums; p23: Mary Evans Picture Library/Francis Frith, Kevin Eaves/Shutterstock; p24: Archive Images/Alamy; p25: Stephen Woodcock/Flickr; p26: Curtis Watt; p28: Trevor Buttery/Shutterstock, Paul Reid/Shutterstock, Tom Oates/Wikipedia, Tom Curtis/Shutterstock; p29: University of Salford Press/Wikipedia, Jonathan Smith/Flickr.

All other images copyright of Hometown World

Every effort has been made to trace and acknowledge the ownership of copyright.
If any rights have been omitted, the publishers offer to rectify this in any future editions.

Written by Tracy J. Holroyd
Educational consultant: Neil Thompson
Local history consultant: John Doughty
Designed by Sarah Allen

Illustrated by Kate Davies, Dynamo Ltd, Virginia Gray,
Peter Kent, John MacGregor, Leighton Noyes and Tim Sutcliffe.
Additional photographs by Alex Long

First published by HOMETOWN WORLD in 2011
Hometown World Ltd
7 Northumberland Buildings
Bath BA1 2JB

www.hometownworld.co.uk

ISBN 978-1-84993-234-9

WOW!

CELT
500 BC

ROMAN
AD 43–410

ANGLO–SAXON
AD 450–1066

VIKING
AD 865–1066

MEDIEVAL TIMES
1066–1485